TROBAIRITZ

{ Other Books By Catherine Owen }

POETRY

Somatic — The Life and Work of Egon Schiele
The Wrecks of Eden
Shall: ghazals
Cusp/detritus: an experiment in ALLEYWAYS
DOG (a collaboration with Joe Rosenblatt)
Frenzy
Seeing Lessons

ESSAYS

Catalysts: Confrontations with the Muse

TROBAIRITZ

BY CATHERINE OWEN

*The amorous subject cannot write his love story himself. Only a
very archaic form can accommodate the event which he declaims
without being able to recount.*
—ROLAND BARTHES

anvil
PRESS

Library and Archives Canada Cataloguing in Publication

Owen, Catherine
    Trobairitz / Catherine Owen.

Poems.
ISBN 978-1-897535-97-4

    I. Title.

PS8579.W43T76 2012   C811'.54   C2012-905380-5

Cover design: Rayola.com
Cover image: Paul Saturley
Interior design: Heimat House
Author photo: Warren Dean Fulton

Represented in Canada by the Literary Press Group.

Distributed in Canada by the University of Toronto Press and in the U.S. by Small Press Distribution (SPD).

The publisher gratefully acknowledges the financial assistance of the Canada Council for the Arts, the Canada Book Fund, and the Province of British Columbia through the B.C. Arts Council and the Book Publishing Tax Credit.

Anvil Press Publishers Inc.
P.O. Box 3008, Main Post Office
Vancouver, B.C. V6B 3X5 Canada
www.anvilpress.com

Printed and bound in Canada

For Chris Matzigkeit,
AKA Lord Jezeus (1981-2010)
first and always.
He who returned me wholly to metal's side.

Also for Hanephi, the dark muse, and others who have
played and supported this fierce genre with or alongside
me in Vancouver, Edmonton & elsewhere in Canada
from 2002-2009: Adamevil, Mvnk, Herod, Judas,
Malachai, Rob Macabre, Jay Highlander, Ophelius, Dan
Scum, Sinned, Goddess, John the Sound Guy,
wendythirteen, Anatolian Wisdom, Infernal Majesty,
Allfather, Zuckuss, Dead Jesus, Soulscar, Musspelheim,
Psychotic Gardening, Myopia, Age of Desolation,
Carrion Spirit, Tyrant's Blood, Begrime Exemious,
Skepsis, Necrobiosis, Hoarfrost, Sonorous Odium, Dire
Omen & the rest of the metal warriors in the world in
the spirit of humour, healing & honouring.
We are the survivors.

NB: All names used in this book are pseudonyms.

I have been to the ruins/& come back with music

Negotiating amongst ghosts is not for the tuneless/the stone ear

Ashes have their own cadence you see/& just because you bury them

Doesn't mean that, underground/they won't keep singing.

It's all about that melody in the end/that gets stuck in the blood

& won't let you/wholly/die.

[after a partial first line by Lucie Brock-Broido]

{ CONTENTS }

PART TWO: THE TROBAIRITZ

PART THREE: THE MEDIEVAL NAMES OF METAL

Autobiography of a Metalhead

They were gods, those early first visions — from the
leather & Maybelline lady-boys Mötley Crüe were, circa
84-87, to the sanatorium grit of Metallica, skanky Ratt,
grim Slayer, Blackie Lawless with his saw-toothed crotch,
Dee Snider's frizz & Spandex —

Shouting at the Devil, entering Sandman, spinning Round
& Round, Raining Blood, Fucking like a Beast, We're not
Gonna Take It Anymore — dark & sexy altars for teenage
Übermensches — spurring me to score a set of drums
after years of violin, then a Peavey T-13

on which Jesus, the lank-haired shredder of St Patrick's,
schooled me in Crazy Train, Iron Man, Breaking the Law
until I dropped out hard, certain I'd be the next Lita Ford &
got caught, instead, by life (sparked still, through all that
time, by Dio, the Scorps, later on Tool, System of a Down)

— yet fast forward to 2001 — when the metal hunger (sub-
merged if not suppressed) struck me again at even heavier
depths, when Emperor, Mayhem, Bathory, Enthroned,
Gorgoroth — too many to list, hit me — this expanding
world encompassing Moonsorrow, Wolfchant, Funeral

Moth, so on & forth, to Dissection, Rotting Christ, My
Dying Bride, that black & doomed terrain in which less pain
flowed than light & joy — and I found Chris (aka Lord
Jezeus), picked up the bass, became the Abbess & have
made, for a decade now, inhuman songs of one kind or
another, desire

for the music never lessening though I see now we are not
gods, that my passion will not silence a critique of the
scene. That despite this, I will play on though odd, the less-
sanctioned sex, anomalous, getting older, an academic, a
poet, not even a beer-drinker — because it is in

my blood: the fierce, purgative, wild, poisoned, pure,
ambivalent, committed ritual metal is — horns, with all
their knowledge of loss — raised high.

Vida: The Comtessa de Dia

The Comtessa de Dia is often reported to have been born
in Die, a town not far from Orange, but it is also said that
her family had long associations with Aurillac through her
great-grandmother, the earliest trobairitz, Tibors. The
Comtessa had many lovers and married, twice, at a young
age, the last time to the aged troubadour Bernart de
Narbonne. Her cansos, however, were composed for the
elusive Arabic troubadour, Senhal Fohlia, whom she loved
without fail as she toiled alongside him in song, if not in
consummation, though the latter fact remains unproven.
She died sometime between 1220 and 1235 after having
born several children and many more poems — some still
chanted today by the joglars of Langue d'Oc.

Vida: Senhal Fohlia

A descendent of the infidels purged in the first Crusade of 1095, the Senhal's lineage can even be traced to the Saracen conquerors of 8th century Occitania. His noble blood and the high quality of his verses, sung and played in Aurillac, Avignon and throughout Langue d'Oc, occasioned much admiration during the latter half of the 12th century and well into the 13th. Taking neither wives, nor siring children, the Senhal was said to have provoked thwarted desire in many, the most famed perhaps being his chaste (or so they say) liaison with the equally gifted Comtessa. Joglars continue to perform their spirited tenson at all the spring votive festivals. It is not known when Senhal Fohlia died.

Part One

Cansos
&
Other Forms
of Adoration

Prelude

In which the Comtessa addresses her Senhal for the first time

you are not mine
so when you walk into the room
I have no claim
to even the slightest witness of your hands

yet there is a language in you
that utters me
as forests are spoken
by their darkness

and in this moment of address
I live
outside silencing bonds
this invisible commerce of touch

you have walked into my room.

Canso of the Core

Only love,
they told me,
that has something
in common with sound

is suited for this form —
a limitation seeming,
at first, mysterious,
particular, and then,

listening to the birds
of winter, I suddenly knew
there is no love
other

than that which does
not carve song
from what was once
ice.

Canso 1

"I feed on joy and youthfulness"
—COMTESSA DE DIA

To speak of he in words who wordless
is like music is hard, who has but a glimpse
of his hand, cast against the strings, a gull
caught upon the horizon, the whole sea in its cry.

Dark, he curves his body's tall clef
over the guitar, hair scrawling its new form of night
upon my mind. What am I to say of he who watches
me sing, then shuns the slightest feather of my skin?

Cruel that they mark this aim as lust, such
an easily scored note, far from the tangled sonatas
the heart cracks its bow so sharp upon. To speak of he
in words is indeed an adamantine act,

this hunter in Aurillac, composer of hunger,
my life's rare wolf.

Canso 2

"I should never have the wish to sing/because the more I sing/the worse it goes for me in love"
　　　　　—Na Castelloza

Sometimes in the black light I see you,
and your whole body speaks of how it is now,

You far from Langue d'Oc. You tell me you are trying
To compose, but that it is hard to gather the notes,

As it is hard to harvest all the wheat. Just when you
Have threshed the piece for infinity, it slips

Back into chaff and you are left with dust
And a longing you can't assuage with lust

Or with anger. I wish you had told me this,
Not with gestures but with your mouth, and

It had been against mine in that moment, your
Confidences like kisses, but you move away

From my gaze, so dark in your solitude, and
Laugh coarsely with your friends

Imagining that you conceal
The knowledge of exile in my love.

Canso 3

"For times to come/I'll tell the plight/I've earned through loving/in excess"
—COMTESSA DE DIA

There is, in the brute dark, one.

One who has not grown calcified
as the black rock from which most men
are formed
with caverns for minds and a cold starlessness
for purpose.

Soft, he came to me from a distance
to speak of how I sing
and while you, when praising,
are like water trickling thin
through the fissures of Langue d'Oc

he is like a flood
sleek & pealing through my flesh
though he does not know this yet
know how I would dance for him at Aurillac,

my hair wild as the shadows
my mouth unbound
against his name.

Canso 4

*"I love him more than anything/mercy and courtliness don't help
me with him/nor does my beauty, or my rank, or my mind/ for I
am every bit as betrayed and wronged/as I'd deserve to be if I
were ugly"*
          —COMTESSA DE DIA

You, my *amic*, new
as the first starred leaves of spring,
who ever taught you about love?

I should never have trusted you
with words; I who have sung so long
sending notes to you with such harvest abandon!

I don't know why I keep falling
into the dark pit of affection —
it only brings me the pain

of a futile trip to the well
at summer's cruelest zenith.
You must become smaller in me now

as a snowflake lost among the snow
that heaps ever higher
in the hollow of the oldest tree.

Canso 5

"With great evil [done to women] you will have great peace."
—RAIMBAUT D'ORANGE

As with a stream, dearest Senhal,
you are always trying to displace me.

By means of stones, in the way of the axe,
you wish to convert my unsettling path

into a common tongue of water, stabbing
flags through every tiny mastery.

That I am rare to you is nothing
except in the joy you claim at the hunt,

the fierce, pale doe that can never truly
escape you — though fleeing, in her side —

your arrows, arresting all the movements
of her blood.

Canso 6

"I have never enjoyed what I love...for I want what
I cannot have"
　　　　　　　　　　　—Guillaume d'Aquitaine

The lakes, my only Senhal,
are blue, their surface, in the spring sun
glitters as if alive,

but you and I never forget
the toxic sand, the absence of fish.
What is the point, you say, of singing

when all will end up ash? As you are
singing you ask this, just as when we fight,
dashing at each other's flesh with our fists,

we are in love with love, not death.

Canso 7

*"Remember that a man can't save himself from cobwebs in
the heart. My life is so delicately balanced. I'm full of joy, then
despair."*
— RAIMBAUT D'ORANGE

That moment in the less-than-light, your eyes
compelled to glow with those small, secret
fires of springtime, body relinquishing its armour,

and my voice speaking love, absurd
or holy as the yellow-green of leaves in a world
long annulled of awe.

So how is it that the first raw bird song
sends me sudden into hiding, the mind
hibernating from the heat that shouldn't

have been told — into the ear of one
who cannot imagine the lily opening
the same time as the rose.

Canso 8

"Il y'a confusion entre j'aime et je chante"
—William Paden

And that's the way I want to leave our love — you
striding hard towards the door at Aurillac, having

touched me all night, light as the ache of a Chinook,
scarcely speaking but to say, at the last quiver of sound —

I'll walk you back to where you came from — but,
knowing I can't trust myself alone with you, faithless

as autumn in my mind, not letting you see me again,
melting away from our past, vanishing

before you can reach me, the carnal impossible as silence
when love & its singing entwine.

Canso 9

"Those who blame me for too often singing would perhaps have the right to do so if it cost them anything. But what stirs me is the pleasure, not the thirst for gain."
—Arnaut Daniel

That it was not at Aurillac, but at a club anonymous,
exotic, outside city limits.

That I had moved away from Langue d'Oc and knew not what country

my tongue now inhabited.

That we lived as one in the music and it stayed our veins with its pulse.

That we were alone, my Senhal, as the gull that flagged its white cry

against all the sky of night.

That I could no longer speak of love without my hands

signing the word into your flesh.

That our mouths like a whole note met and that

I was your Comtessa, one moment in the vast

lamp-wilderness of stars.

Portrait of a Troubadour

I wish forever to see him standing there, lionized
above me in the humble light and all
his poise, his posture, though that would not
honour the way he walks, his stature in the streets,
his dark stride bare, and if I had this I would not
have his voice, the tone so spare and rich, and who
I ask, could hold his music?

Never will they invent an instrument
to clasp his flesh in this moment as he
tall & impossible as longing stands, his
naked chest, his hair unbinding
down his back and I
incapable of keeping him breath with words.

The Comtessa Meets Her Senhal in a Dream

You walked into the room, my only one, folded
in your arms, a cat — but not full grown — a kitten
smaller than a lute, smooth on its haunches as wood,
the rest all furred and dark and with it
you carried a bowl.

In the bowl, you told me, was milk, warm
honey and the newest milk, and as the petal
of her tongue licked, you grew within me
as a plant and there was no
animal inside our love
but roots that laved my walls

while the kitten all the time was calm
her mouth barely rippling the skin
as the milk lapped down.

Canso 10

*"I must sing of what I do not want, I am so angry with
the one I love."*
— Comtessa de Dia

How could winter have come so soon
and you who lay your body over mine —
a moon reflected in a lake —

be such another season?
With words you drew me, with music,
your body dark as the thunder's passage

and when I wept
it was like Avignon in the springtime.
Now the petals of my stories

are frozen and the lips that let them
fall thinking you, tormentor,
a friend, are cold.

I cannot breathe against
your life's sudden ice,
the puzzle of glass upon your heart.

Canso 11

"I wonder at how you have become so proud, Friend, towards me, and I have reason to lament; it is not right that another love take you away from me."
—COMTESSA DE DIA

She tells me to ignore your seasons,
a whole year surfacing in a day,
your winter often twice,
but for a lone crocus in the frost,

I wait.

She tells me to dismiss your landscapes,
deserts & oceans colliding,
but for one line of birds
on your horizon,

I wait.

Canso 12

*"I take comfort because I never did anything wrong, Friend,
towards you, in anything, rather I love you more than Seguin
did Valensa (mythical lovers)."*
                              —Comtessa de Dia

As a shooting star, Senhal,
you must be to me, a star witnessed,
when looking out to sea,

by the eye's thinnest edge,
that the star seems not to fall
it falls so fast, but

as a trail laves its light
across the mind
in a million-year-old path,

the death that has long happened,
received by us
as love.

Canso 13

"O beautiful dark one...before he greets me, he bids me farewell"
—Arabic troubadour al Tutili (c. 1126)

If I could stop opening my throat, Senhal,
to sing of what is not — like a bird in a wasteland
filling the air with forests
I would

for what does it bring me
this obsession
but an ache around the heart so ancient
that it is the bark of the oldest tree.

In the meadow
there is a bee whose legs light
rampant on the darkest thistle
until pollen haloes its thighs

how I fear I won't release you
as long as music is your pollen
and the thistle
your mind.

Canso 14

"I know it's easier to lose than gain; still, though I be blamed,
I'll tell the truth"
—Azalais de Porcairages

No desire without tension
(you tell me)

that the ocean at Dauphiné needs cliffs
or else the salt flood would devour the town

(all its edicts   all those battlements)
and then

(what then?)
only rubble of our love and not this sweet

unyielding endless scarce-succumbing
between us

would you want this
(o would you?)

(o would you

The Comtessa Imagines
Her Senhal at Labour

At first, she had thought him content, turning
wood ancient with paint & a lathe,
insulated against the grain
breathing solitude's varnish,
even a counterpart to his music
in which the new was also made myth.

But now she knows how the hours hunched
over a bench, sanding away the gloss
on a high-priced divan   body masked
against the fumes
fills him with hate for the fakery
in such work

and is nothing like the way his art draws
from a thousand years of lineage
and, with a dark finish, hears it new.

The Comtessa Sleeps, Chastely, with Her Senhal & His Domna

You invite us in, calling us family, she
who has sacrificed a country to love you, I knowing only
language's exile, the watcher.

We do not hold each other.

I, who had wept once over this, wanting to hold you both,
and been denied do not, now I have the chance,
hold you (o the unaddressed complexity of happiness!)

For hours, our limbs burn like memory, heat
from the day's sun laquering the walls, lacing
our urge to stir against each other's flesh.

Or perhaps there is no ache, finally, as we become
infant in the night, against the peacock feathers
of your quilt the feet I last, in frenzy, kissed,

innocent in amniotic light, the toe of one
upon the other's crease.

Senhal Fohlia Sends the Comtessa an Instant Message in the Form of an Unwitting Haiku

Did I say anything.
Snowing already?
Bacardi & I.

Canso 15

"If only I could lie beside you for an hour and embrace you lovingly"
—Comtessa de Dia

Hearing of the *epreuvé*, chastity's test,
where a sword, unsheathed, is slid

between two naked people in bed
and all night they must remain

on either side of its steel, that hard,
mineral ridge dividing them, flesh

not touching, and in the morning,
if the blade has not been shifted

and their skin is un-mouthed
by the edge then, and only then,

will their love be deemed pure,
a courtly union unmarred by animal lusts

you said — *do we dare?*
(for to fail would mean one word of pleasure

and many thereafter of silence

Amor de Lonh: Love Intensified by Distance

They knew long winters there.
Ice drawing its hard face over the moat.
Then the longer drought times of war.
White & red of men leaving.
How little we have learned to suffer.

Secrets that remain in this room.
The ones of flesh, the burning ones.
But can I lie felled for centuries like Heracles?
All the harsh dust of Nemrut Dagi.
Beyond Hope, the lushness of forests.

In your language, it is the "mountain of pain".
In mine, the place of release.
Not even a dove between these words.
Longing still crests within me.
We are ghosts, after all.

Yet if we could have been chaste forever.
What an epic of missing.

*

What an epic of missing.
This, being chaste forever.
We are ghosts, after all.

Longing still crests within me —
Not even a dove between these words
In mine, the place of release is your language —
The mountain of pain beyond hope

All the lushness of forests, the harsh dust of Nemrut Dagi
Where I lie felled for centuries like Heracles
Or the ones of flesh, the burning ones.
The secrets that remain in this room?

How little we have learned to suffer:
White & red of men, leaving.
The long drought times of war.
Ice drawing its hard face over the moat

The longer winters.

Canso 16

for the Domna Assag or Love Test

*"But she knows my sorrow and my pain/and when it pleases her,
she gives me comfort and honours me, and when it pleases her, I
make do with less"*
—Bernart de Ventadorn

There is one condition: darkness.
Then the Kalamata light of her flesh,
her name's difficult spices.

Suddenly she is naked as a perfect seed
and you do not know why
she is embracing you, why

her mouth's small rupture finds yours
or your hands the sleek clay of her breasts.
He is watching us both

like someone at the site of a collision
helpless in the beauty of accidents
but when she calls for him to join us

he is already in our arms
as if our bodies are the only room.
Then she is gone

and he is entering me from behind
like someone praying, as in those dreams
where I had imagined him, wet and bent

over my back, hair working its rivulets
into skin and I know somewhere she is
listening, our cries translated by night

but she never once tears us apart —
I thinking this is her gift.
How wrong I was.

Comjat

for F.B. (1974-2003)

Back when you were breathing, she
took this picture, the one photo in which she

wasn't there. It was of you sleeping, you
without your mouth moving, rare, in the blue

light of the near-dawn room. She who drew
so much more and less than I did from you,

she who was your muse and in this photo turned
your body, unbroken, and in its dream, burning

to an image I with my thousand, unquenched
poems have not, the dark bearings
of your hair cut hard against the pillow, inched
away from you, limbs freeing

only enough distance to sketch your lashes, shearing
light from your skin, its ashes wrenched
from future urns, a moment black & white & clenched
against all I since have learned of leaving.

Canso 17

"E tenc per flor lo conglapi" (I take hail to be a flower)
—RAIMBAUT D'AURENGA

When, Senhal, did I become
so accustomed to winter?
There is no us my first hard fall
into cold, such ice still a violence

though your utterance in the end
made sense.
I held a summer in my mind
until then.

Now there is snow in every nest,
and when I wake I expect
my gardens
to be white.

So close have I grown to December
that if spring were ever to come
I would distrust
its beauty, its word

thawing open on my tongue
and would swallow hard,
praying for the hail
I love.

Canso 18

*"Since I war against you and yet cannot even approach you,
And neither flee you, nor satisfactorily give chase"*
—RAIMON JORDAN

You were a storm last night in my mind,
one of our new winters,
and all the trees in your arms blew down,

so little soil in my dream.
And yet too you persist in summer,
where I cannot sleep for remembering

the heat you thrust sharp in my skin
and the way the evenings felt longer
in the gentle clock of your hands.

How I want you to speak one season
though terrible — such killing for peace.

Canso 19

"That's why you have such power over me
I'll come running when you call"
          —ANON. 12TH CENTURY

Responding to me,
your body,
as it always does
though your hands
never stir on my surfaces,

the longest night of the year, I,
wanting to hold you do,
and cannot,
the wild field of flowers
within what you call the nothing

that is your flesh
waiting inside silence
and for this, more beautiful
the scythe lifting always
on the edge of us

though we are trembling
from something other
than fear.

Escondig

*"It has always been my lot never to have joy of what I loved...
for I knowingly do many things of which my heart tells me: It's
all pointless."*
                    —GUILEM DE PEITEU

As the snow persists in falling
and the thaw will not be mine
so it is

that silence has become a season.
You have not left me
but my apologies for keeping you

in my mind's stifling tower room.
If you are dream, let you remain so.
If memory, I have no hold on you.

What was scripted will not be eternal
but ash.
Perhaps if we do not speak

it will be best
and your forgiveness
that never would have shone as words

can become a glance
burning my contrition to lies

as I return it with every breath

incapable of regret
even now.

How to Be a Domna

You do not have to give
but of your image

and it must be stark, trellised,
a wrought button of velvet,

a carefully cinctured mouth.

You need know nothing
but the strict richness of indifference.

You need be nothing
but a never-melting absence

a hard snow of flesh
on the mind of one who waits, senselessly,

for your language, a tongue
that can speak yes, but seeks

the finer silk of silence, for you
need not respond. You need not hear the songs.

There is nothing you must do.

Canso 20

"But what I desire is denied me. Ah damn the godfather who put upon me this curse to love and not be loved!"
    —Jaufre Rudel

Warning you not to be cold after you, hard
held me, I have already witnessed
your winter.

Dividing love from desire —
nothing new —
there is a history to this knife

but each time I grip the blade
backwards
in my own endless narrative of blood.

Will there ever be a century
when seasons end without the tragic
and leaves fall, passive

becoming little boats for snow.

Canso 21

He "is the citadel of my worth...joy from others is not worth an apple to me"
—ARNAUT DANIEL

Against the cliffs at Saintonge
the Pacific Ocean rails
and gulls like vivid foam
fly up
avid for krill in the boat's wake.

Do you watch me where I long?
February's harsh light,
uncertain of how to stream after
the rain's season of darkness,
echoes this awkward pose.

Where do I stand?
How do I endure?
Arching over the prow —
a figurehead of blood —
I gaze down to where the foam

as with lichen's erosion of a tomb
melts away our passage.
Yet I have words with which to gift you,
words for the water's mouth
and the night of the world.

Canso 22

*"…nor did a time ever arrive, sweet, handsome friend, when I
didn't want to see you often, nor did I ever feel regret"*
                    —TIBORS (earliest trobaritz fragment)

Will you sing about my hands,
you said,
the watchmen in Carcassonne
signalling us to part
from the night's rare heat
held in its solitude
like a swamp orchid.

How can I tell you
what will find language?
Is there a word
for every moment
you entered me
or is there only this
happiest of silences

this slipping
through a dawn of forests
dew cresting
against my feet.

Canso 23

I, who came from a soft, green land, how
can I claim this winter as my own
where only the magpie knives
above the hardened river
and shadows hew stains on the ice.

When it has gifted me with all, how
could I have betrayed rain's constant embrace
that has never asked of me while giving, damp
in its blindness, as laughter, for this

cold stranger and his song —
the snow that I harbour on my tongue
and that I have taught, in its turn,
how to warm me.

Canso 24

"Love of a distant land, for you all my heart aches."
—Jaufre Rudel

How do I know, most wholly,
there is home in you,
not my liege,
and of a distant land.

How when I hold you
does all this foreign and yes impossible
lose consequence
or desert.

How does a fingernail
traced down the nape of a neck
become compass and thus
irrefutable

and our flesh, pressed
to the place of song
how beyond
this castle.

Canso 25

*"I don't know why you're always on my mind, for I've searched
from good to evil your hard heart, and yet mine's unswerving."*
—NA CASTELLOZA

If I could live forever in a land of snow
it is only because
in the barren alder
is you, and in the relentless crusts of ice —

you, in the cold cries birds make
from the ciphers of their nests, and you in
the difficult movements
through the drifts that crest

endless from Dauphiné
which is not to say that any
of this is not beautiful,
also, of course, reminding me

of you.

Canso 26

*"Since I first caught sight of you, I've been at your command;
and yet, friend, it's brought me naught, for you've sent
neither messages nor envoys."*
— Na Castelloza

*"Give me one word from you that says: I have seen you
beneath your blue skin."*
— Diana Brebner

Days drag, my Senhal, and from you,
nothing

(o to expect a crocus from the frost...
Others send me letters ripe

with gardens of language
but what of this do I care to harvest?

Then, on the day of spring's hopelessness,
suddenly — a word!

Those who rave about my beauty
on amethyst-scented pages are

meaningless as ice against
the light of this one syllable

in which I bathe as the sun in April
though it revert to grey tomorrow

and the temperature of your silence
drop.

Canso 27

*"Why did you become a lover, since you leave
all the suffering to me?"*
                              —ANON.

Terrible,
in my dream,
not to know you.

Like a language
grown strange
with the saying,

I have spoken you
too many times
and you've become nightmare

as an over-tilled field
feeding me stones.
How, after all, not

to know you — when once
uttering your name
was everything

when the lexicon of yes
leant sunshine its multiple words
for warmth.

Canso 28

"I want to know the truth about the love we two once had, so tell me, please, why you've given it to someone else."
—ISABELLA

Wrought what
these songs, O Senhal,
En & Na no longer
but two brooks flowing

hard & parallel, guilt
casting leaves on their banks.
And dead you've been
and prison

this touch no longing, no
window, the notes I've lit
less sun than those dreams
you've leant me of dark

where you are lightly
with other women
flickering as false spring
while I sit winter

and alone.

Canso 29

"Handsome friend, as a lover true, I loved you ... but now I see
I was a fool."
—Castelloza

No longer of snowfalls
will I write, lost Senhal,
now seeing not solely your winter

but how I've served it, most painfully,
as my season.
Why would I hold to what melts

and more, what provides
no shelter, but is brute
and lacking in bird song.

There is no endlessness
to this suffering —
you are not one of spring's wildflowers

that I cannot choose to stop loving
despite knowing
no love is spared me.

Canso 30

*"Joy and youth were the essential qualities of any courtly love —
male or female."*
                    —MEG BOGAN

Desiring that desire
not be
in the way the heart

old in its season, does

I went out into the world
and did not want.

For moments,
I did not want, worn
by the winter of your face.

For moments,

I was ice and wanted only calm.
And then, in the way spring

is known, so that snow remains
one does not see snow, he
who is young, his laughter

a land of silk, looked up
and the green in that look
and the wheat, swallows

tightening & loosening their flight

over the fields.

Canso 31

"I court the man who's brought me grief."
—CASTELLOZA

If there were a spell
to send you far from me
I would sing it
but there have been
so many notes
and none
have swept my dreams
clean of you
with the hard necessity
of an autumn wind.

And though I speak
not of missing you
you are violent in me
as the sight of mountains
after the immeasurable
desert, cold,
without solace
as love.

e Comtessa Sees a Photograph of Senhal Fohlia When He Was a Child

Blond the small flint of your hair
body on your grandmother's shoulders
hands curving fast on her ears
the pale, live shells of your palms
her back hunched into your squirming
as your eyes darken like olives.
There is something you have not been given
this eternal outing on the Bosphorus
your lip upon the other in a wave
crashing salt on the impossible world.

Canso 32

"If I'm sad and mournful, it's because you don't remember me."

—CASTELLOZA

After the windstorm, Senhal
there is still a forest,
you are right in this
but not that
I will ever walk through it again
without recalling where green
arched high
in place of rootlessness.

I would never wish
for these hard clearings
where dense & redolent cedars
grew
even though the light
has released a sapling
pear blossoms striking their white
and quieter stars.

Trobar Clus

*"But I wonder/where your heart is/for its house and hearth/
are hid and you won't tell"*
        —Lombarda

*"One esteems gold more than salt, and with any song,
it is the same."*
        —Raimbaut d'Aurenga

Who was on the streets of my body you
words that were old no
longer a market where
slight fish linger beside oranges.
You are cobbled, wainscoting, slip-shod.
There is a dark indeed in me, a little
yes on feet.
Why have I traveled to your language,
crawling, scrimping
on light and the oil in your eyes
silent.
Settlements have no origins
where floods scurry
their blood-utterances
and you are not
this yield.

Fals d'Amour

"But he who knows how to speak well and does so is indeed among the chosen for he can, if he wishes, regain consciousness of himself."
— MARCABRU

Would you immerse yourself in foetid swamps   embrace
murk   and call it love   name it sacred
this land of   pitch & ragweed   sing devotion
to a stone?

Then why obsess about his loss?

He gives you nothing   you have not dreamed.

His ice,
his blooms,
his snow,
his leaves   are but visions of your throat

and this gold & glorious flesh   this Langue d'Oc that he was
was not and less than these words that trail like keening birds west,

vanishing   from the earth.

The Rival

"The troubadours' self-referential quest for beauty and perfection"
—WILLIAM PADEN

In front of me
she sat down on the toilet
drunk on snuck-in Smirnoffs
at the metal show's hiatus

and I saw the innocent
question mark of her tampon string
swinging beneath the soft-rust
strip of pubic hair

and all the time she was laughing
(just a groupie, fan, girlfriend)
red curls foaming around her tailbone, around
the fine, white points of her hips

nothing but a *res*, lost Senhal
she washing her lilies in the sink
I *gileos*   spurned.

Canso for Domna Bieris

the only trobairitz to write a canso addressed to a woman,
the Lady Maria, in the early 13ᵗʰ c.

As birds sing in the ice, so I was singing
to you, Domna
though I had not the language of thaw
and my prison, un-melting.

Gaiety and happiness were but masks,
the skin of a false springtime —
I heard you chanting from afar,
like flowers your sighs were parting

but still the dark suitor beckoned
gift of another season
a vos mas coblas man
though toward him like snow I turn.

On Seeing Photographs of the Domna Following the Loss of Senhal Fohlia

Angle One:
tiny in your bustier
silver legs sealed
a stoic for what was holy
I who touched him
watch you in miniature
we were neither of us loved

Angle Two:
when he on his pedestal
had dazzled us
with the thinnest of gifts:
you a platter of oranges,
a language, me even less
than this, what strange
soft fools of lust.
now you are metallic,
by grieving, ghosted
from the back only
the shimmering plate
of a bass-viol, unfinished,
and yet he plays on you

and you do not want him to,
while I become
conductor of silence

Angle Three:
then he leaves, the beloved
and you are strangers
in the span of a day,
years melting, like your body,
to an unyielding ore.
we are both betrayers here —
he a lost liege and I his
Comtessa of absence.
you forgive me, you repeat
but your face is turned aside,
hair sharply combed (three or four strands
dead as spears against your cheek)
and your lips runneled old by old weeping.

Angle Four:
you had not wanted it —
the child — yet it was there
all the same
and leeched from you
like some ancient chancre
it still blinked its brown eyes
in your dreams
there was nothing he could do
about this (what can I do he
kept railing) until you became
what you
had not kept.
I would have thought
you were a fetus, your hairless,
starved flesh knotting
into its darkness
de-wombed onto a pure black sheet
and the paraphernalia of capture
all around you.

Angle Five:
from this throat no
singing   no time no
nothing digestible
stomach wincing into a fist
why like his myth
could he not
sacrifice.
your face in a blur of agony
neck so nakedly thrust up
to what, in the end,
is suffering.
camera an asp plucked
hard from its basket
but not even death in it
just two red entrances
imperceptible, closing.

The Last Canso: An Unraveling Corona

"I love you without regret, but love has stung me with such force."
—Castelloza

"It's a season of storms. My love's not altered!"
—Maria Solaladeira, aka Erin Mouré

There is no end to seasons, Senhal.
How could you think it so?

Believing this, your mind's battlements
vast, you are beyond my touch, straining

its warmth through your winter
until ice rides the sun.

She is the one who still summers
you with language.

When I left, guilty with the luxury
of sleep, her leg had found your waist,

its slim, olive hinge clipped above
your pelvis, all the vulnerable light

liquid on your face, and your feet —
a lie of nakedness.

*

Your feet a lie of nakedness I
have nothing left to give you.

Masks pass like traffic across
your face and I am insane when

I look on you with love, sick
when I speak to you.

These are your names for fear.
Why did I ever imagine we held

each other? Like ice beneath the slaving
of sun's winter, this thaw you

annihilate with nightfall.

*

This thaw you annihilate with nightfall
where, lying beside you, burning.

Outside the window, crows open the ocean
with their cries, mountains fasten into shadows;

she, dark with transparent dreams.
The old romance shivers, that myth

refashioned by exile. I want you I do not
want you and what do you want

you say — my ice become lies in day's sun?

*

You *say my ice becomes lies in day's sun,*
the sharp water softening to language, ice

and the sun no kin, but raw, Comtessa, in their
antipathies, or is this what I heard in my dream

as with the Domna's pale country you slept,
all that I had sung but a silence, and this

impossible pollen beyond.

*

And the impossible pollen beyond you
is you, without her slim olive hinge, a sun

straddling ice…o how I watch you both,
a still life of leaving each other —

the beauty before waking into strangeness.
You say that part of us has passed, Senhal,

when notes wrote us into flesh, but it is fear
in which your coldness forgets, as I learn

your country's salt tongues like a key
to a ruined door.

*

Your country's salt tongues no key to a ruined door
for though I fall asleep in your country

I wake, after all, in my own, dust
for your syllables, ice for those ancient

suns. She is no one's and I am not yours.

*

Though she is no one's and I cannot be yours
how many times have I named you winter

strained to silence you as ice and her,
your falling sun.

I will never again know you as sleepers.
The slim, olive hinge of her leg, your feet

unburied in the light, and I leaving
before true dawn, you scarcely

recalling my song, though I have told you
there is no end to seasons.

The Reason: A Partimen Starring the Domna, Senhal Fohlia and the Comtessa

DOMNA:

As spring moves far from winter
and blossoms repel ice
so I no longer wish to share your company,
neither you, Senhal,
lover of the darkest *forfeitz,*
nor you Comtessa,
whose *cons* brings such despair.

SENHAL:

But I do not understand, Domna
as in my love I remain faithful!
It was she who told me of the tree of knowledge
and shaped my desire for the apple, not
I who am to blame for the verse
upon her tongue, nor the night
in my human arms, not I the offender.

COMTESSA:

Weak & foolish Muse!
If I am *marritz* it is only
in the honesty I've shown
all those poems of devotion
and my mouth upon your skin.

And you, Domna, though
I've been *falhir* in our amity
I was faithful to art and its needed
protest of adultery, you
who were wed to a man
noble in his mien, if base in words
should be glad he birthed such tributes
from a voice as strong as mine!

DOMNA:

But I wanted him as my own
and you, my confidante
and now I have nothing, and
both of you are bereft
so what was the point of your singing?

COMTESSA:

You are simple, my queen
when it comes to the realm of verse.
I did not have a choice
in which lord fathomed my heart
as the moon cannot persist in darkness.

For me there is no hearth and no
silence but serving as witness to love
and its holy music.

SENHAL (*to himself*):

Her gifts were pure, it is true, and if it were not
for those *lauzengiers*, I would be free
of derision, free to share my fidelity with two.

DOMNA:

Heretic and *jogleresa!*
My affections were heaven-bound.
Your lusts but mortal gasps of earth.

COMTESSA:

So be it.
I am called to chant of what is
my only regret that all cannot grasp
such devotion
and consign my rare chorus
to the night.

Devinalh on the Domna

Who is the object of all affection
& the giver of none?

Who in remaining clothed
becomes more naked than the nude?

Who is song personified
& yet silence embodied?

Who in serving as ruler number one
is, at the same time, the zero subject?

Who wears both a gown
& a suit of armour?

Who is lauded for both her physical curves
& her moral lines?

Who is equal parts flesh, absence
& a game played among men?

Who is what is not that is everything?

Cansos of One Year After

*"You stayed a long time, friend, and then you left me, and it's a
hard, cruel thing you've done."*
                                              —LOMBARDA

"And it grieves me that we've been so long apart."
                                              —ANON. 12TH C

Birds begin their nests
from February's first thaw
so confident are they in spring
hopeful for an above-zero world
but I have lost my instincts,
Senhal,
I who hurried to nest in you
after slow seasons of longing
was given one warm night of melting
one alone
and then morning arrived with its ice
and the nests in my mind
were abandoned.

        *

But why seek to nest
when never a sign to take shelter
unreliable beyond a smile, desire's
acknowledgement.

I could have burned with you
for years, Senhal
if not for the error birds
make at melting —
ice was not a prior state
my flesh had urged to spring,
it would return,
and I foolish with my blossoms
of words in your winters.

*

What that night was,
against all the imagined nests,
was enough, my Senhal.
How than worth everything
could it be less —
your lips, your eyes, the fire of your arms
around me, the way you
gathered up my hair, no *gardadors*
near us.

*

And yet *mezura* in love
is hard.
For I who wanted you whole & ever
this year is a length of winters
though I claim another season
in the dark.

The Comtessa Sees Her Senhal in a Dream a Year beyond the Likelihood of Them Ever Meeting Again

Do the details matter anymore, lost Senhal?
Whether I called you David or Raimbaut,

if my gifts were a horoscope, heart's ease,
a mirror, if

when I placed the laurel of night on your head
you looked pleased or scornful?

That I dream of you is sign enough of vigil
: my heart attendant in the dark

beyond all these castle walls
and distance, able to

conjure up love and its witnesses
though the light will not let

them testify
nor the truth.

Part Two

The
Trobairitz

Tenso: Between the Comtessa de Dia and Senhal Fohlia, circa 1186

"I know this is a fitting thing for me/though everybody says it isn't proper for a lady to plead her case with a knight"
—CASTELLOZA

RAZO (sung by the joglar Tornada)

"Doubtless, my dear audience, you have heard of the Comtessa and how, along with a favoured visage, the gods have gifted her with the unquestionable power of song, a gift, some say, that has enabled her to speak her mind more readily than some of her sex are wont to do. In such fashion, troubled by the fabled Senhal Fohlia's resistance, not only to her indisputable charms, but more importantly, to her rightful place as a singer in the court of Aurillac, she has invited the Senhal, most graciously, to engage in a tenson with her on the ageless debate regarding a woman's role in an art that has long been performed by men on a public stage. The Senhal, fresh from the success of his canso — Maiso ni borda no vei ("My house and hearth are hid") seeks to convince the Comtessa that she is fortunate among her sex and need not even raise the question, but the Comtessa's rage prevails, as we will hear from her exclamatory provocation to the unyielding end."

COMTESSA:

One woman to twenty men! Or only one singing in all of Langue d'Oc, one in Saragossa or St. Cinq, one in Valentinois, Saintonge, one in her citadel playing alone, composing her songs whilst all around her servant girls scrub floors, ladies engage in beauty's set rituals, babies wail other women's names.

Why is this, prince of the given stage?

SENHAL:

My only Miels de Domna, for what reason do you bemoan your
fate? You should feel grateful that the courtly doors have opened
for you and even famous men attend your shows (though not
without grumbling, at times, of your affronts).

COMTESSA:

When it is just I in the light I am not breaking the form,
not casting back the mold but merely slipping a fissure into a
wall of sounds woven with my sex at the core, shrunken to one
body amid the millions, one rose-common mind in place of
multitudinous blooms.

SENHAL:

You perform with the men, my lady, I cannot see what disgrace
there is in this when surely it is a triumph for your sex to suffer.

COMTESSA:

Acceptance, yes, O Senhal, has come hard and in any case
is not what I ask — to be gathered into a group all droning at once
in secret tongues is of no real interest to me. What I'm trying to say
is that an isolated *femme* is only revolution's ache and thus no more
than an exotic beast trapped within a cage of dogs.

SENHAL:

What need for revolution in a song that already survives
on the edge of society, that toils its cansos underground, only
a note in a thousand drawing the attention of a patron or the crowd!

COMTESSA:

So you see then how it is wrong for such a scene to exclude
the very blood of its making?

SENHAL:

Foolish woman, we are caught by what promises to stay silent, a quiet
beauty is our net, the domna who slips her form behind the veil of a
castle's casements. How can you expect me to sing of you
when you lunge all over my mind, pawing at my thoughts like a wolf!

COMTESSA:

Did I ever choose to be your Belhs Deportz — to be one of the
many for whom passivity delights and subjugation is the greatest
gift of all?

SENHAL:

Can you not just stick to the words offered you as speech? I am
content within *my* lexicon. Say it! Moon, midnight, pale ladies,
endless war, all histories fixed and perfect, ancient verities —
why must you add the word "why" in there, have domnas
on fire, forests outside the axe, other planets of our language —
what fidelity is this?

COMTESSA:

Your posturing is a trick, turning you as a puppet to your own
constant strings. Fidelity is where I was born, yet it is plain that we
define it separately, one as a child and one a crone. Can you not
enlarge your rote forms?

SENHAL:

All religions have their symbols, *belle dame*, and comport their
rituals within a structure immutable to the centuries. There
is no need to alter a functioning and lovely thing — *you* have
squeezed inside its doors.

COMTESSA:

I will tear those doors from their hinges, those carefully
polished paeans to fear! There is room for many more windows in
your edifice of steel. The singer is she who will not be bound, not
to a stove, not to a child, never to the rigid properties of
her sex as you, though you create tales of swords, refuse to go
to war because it is your art to whom you hold homage, not
the court's, the king's glory.

SENHAL:

This does not make me womanly!

COMTESSA:

No surely, God forbid! But it is the androgyne in us who sings,
the one who will not be confined — as much as you praise
prisons you are as open as the wind!

SENHAL:

I did once concede to this, did I not?

COMTESSA:

Yes, I believe, but in private, when there posed no threat
to your manhood, yet when the others were present,
parading their muscular texts around the room, swaggering
their sex, you assumed their stance and, when I called you
on your admission, refused to grant what I had heard from
your lips, denying like Peter his Jesus until the third cock crew.

SENHAL:

But it is to that world I owe allegiance, them the bread in my mouth,
not you.

COMTESSA:

Your truth is sad, beloved singer still, for our art sends us
no such reins and we who leash the lion will only ever be
throwing meat to mice.

Three Portraits of Trobairitzes in Chansonniers

Rod

When I was growing up it was still
"spare the rod and spoil the child"
for the shaft-backed nuns shipped
from Chicoutimi to rot
in the convent school off Main.

The rod, punishment, from 1150 on
carefully refinished as correction,
a shining thing.

But you, not soft, an offshoot
of that pedestal, that *taciturnas* realm
are painted here as

wielder,

your cultured hands upon the oar that
in 1902 would be defined as "penis"
and you, the castrator.

Scepter

Royal, always, mistress of a fief,
married to a man for the smooth
sundown of his hands, not his land's wealth,

you chose to salute the traveler, circa 1300,
who wanted you to prop up his fortunes
by spinning you on the wheel of his cansos.

Scepter only became "shaft" in 1950,
alluding to unfair treatment, suggesting
the act of sodomy, but it is this

he painted on your lips, twisted sharp
in your own hard song to the most
common medieval noun — "offense."

Falcon

Though bird, this is no
beating heart at your wrist, leashed

by the hooks to your tiny, patrician
bones. The shape of its wings renders it sickle and,

in 1250, brought from Rome, its feathers
reaped your absolute fields

and your poems were sheaves of its singing.
He has painted you master here, but

by 1250 Béziers had been burned and you
were no rapturous keeper.

Alba

Waking, rare, before the first light
lips the battlements, razes

the lost realm with fire &
stirring, behind the curtain

annuls this silence with children
& the day's same din.

Beginning, a neighbourhood of birds,
the land's true denizens, robin,

finch & wren, their confederacy androgyne
in the cedars and cherry blossoms

of my small orchard where no *pastorelas*
will be sung, no hushed shepherdesses

seduced by the brute owner of this estate but
in his car turning past towards work

see only my face, cast in raw frost, mouth
thawing the notes that rise

as kin to the sun.

Neumes (2002)

She had bought the bass in a pawn shop, a red Vantage
hanging above the corpses of acoustics, glass cases crammed
with the ticking of stolen watches. When the owner handed
it to her over the counter, it was more terrible than when her
child had been slotted into her adolescent arms, so many
years ago, its body ridging beneath her pebble-heavy breasts.
Yet she was supposed to feel right with that weight, that
shape against her, its sanctioned pose. With the bass, there
were no such blessings.

It had been formed for a height, a breadth not hers, though
somehow she would learn how to hold it, mold her fingers to
muscular slabs, press pipes into her biceps, sculpt a hard
stance from her thighs. Within eleven weeks, she had taken
to the stage as if doubt was only reserved for the immortal.

Once she had snipped a sliver off her son's ear when he had
whipped his head quickly against a hair cut's imperative; once
long after, she will fail to catch her bass when it falls like a
glass-struck bird from its case onto the asphalt. To illusions
of possession there are always reproaches —

the small blank eyes of scars staring at their maker.

Gileos

Females in the metal sub-culture are "divided between those who dress like boys and those who try to emulate the bitch goddesses they see in [metal] videos...heavy metal is masculine and women who want to become members of the metal subculture must do so on male terms."
—PHILIP BASHE & DEENA WEINSTEIN

The matriarch in the metal scene was once her camp counselor. At a Catholic camp, of course, a clump of trailers and tee-pees on the shores of Gabriola, complete with a swimming beach where she earned pink ribbons for Must Not Wade Alone, her body thrashing in the salt, thin and given to hypothermia. The counselor was nine years older, too tall for her to remember what she looked like later, just a presence of warm hormones, capable of taking her seriously as they straggled down the trails, speaking forgotten philosophy as everyone else sang "Blue Moon."

She wrote letters to her for months as the terrors of Grade 3 began and received a reply to them, once, the signature a giant loop encompassing all she then sensed of womanhood. Full throttle ahead to 2001, when, raw to the Vancouver scene, she is invited to her house for a beer. Unaware, of course. The counselor, now styling herself The Countess, sits on her leopard print couch, staring. The next morning she gets a call, "I know who you are! Little Kitty, right? The Padre? Camp Lalache?" When she wonders where the seven-year-old is in her face, the Countess cries, "Eyes and teeth — they never change."

*

The Countess and Ms Twelve are the hardcore world's two goddesses. Both in their 40s, single mothers, un-redeemably tough. Ms Twelve is tougher though as, despite owning a condo, she slaves in a skanky pub seven nights a week, and flaunts a Mohawk, while the Countess dons white and assists dentists in a Victoria Drive office. Fond of slagging each other for their differences, seeking superiorities, as women have been trained to do. So catching sight of her, one calls "cutie," while the other glares — unable to deal with one of their own kind in a realm where fierce women bear the brand of the diamond-eyed Dodo.

*

She once gave head to Corpsebanger after their Studebaker's show. She appeared in a video as Loki's grease-clad dancer. She gained infamy when, drunk at a party, she thrust a beer bottle up her cunt to the rhythm of "Tit-fucked by TINTIN." She became Bondage Babe of the Week on Disciple's S&M website. She donned a monster mask and bounced her hard breasts for a Powerskanks launch. She may even have sung, but in a shirt so thin and a skirt so short her body was the only heard note in the grind core/thrash/death metal band. She simply wasn't and the stage teemed with men.

Eneug 1

Hating the stench of the undigested, relegated cellars,
beer scrim on all the tables, hating the wrecked red carpet,
the lost-toothed patrons lumbering off their bar stools,
Hating their paw-fulls of sticky coins, the cheap, cheap
swill & butts glutting the toilets,
Hating the twittering girls, their apropos tatties,
stabbed tongues that clack against their chatter,
tits that shrink men's eyes to bite-sized leers, the dirty,
pretty, plump and pale teens, twirling their youth
in my face, hating the youth youth youth of it, the
anthemed, apocalyptic air of the thick & pitiful mosh
pit with its bashing, pumping hurls of flesh and the asshole
who asks my sign, lynching a ridiculous cowboy hat
beneath an unscriptable bit of beard.

Plazer 1

So much love for the vulnerable!

The just legal who sparkle with being perfectly
new to it all, the 9$ pitchers a paean to justice,
eternity evident in a catcall and the absolute
socialism of the pit.

Love too for the deaf busser, his crescent moon
jawline and gentle scrag of hair — the oldest
dishwasher you'll meet, stacking the glasses
in plastic slots, tossing down the dregs

and love too

For Jim, with his Prince Caspian mop, this
subtle engineer of noise, patch cords lassoing
his arms, band shirt tipped with sweat.

Love is also in the Lemon Drop cure for an abscess, a tiny
bright shot of it, New Year's Eve and the lead singer

strutting around the floor, his skin a silk flower, impervious to all.

Eneug 2

For the man in the I Love Strippers shirt, hate,
and hate too for the subtlety of words lost between
the smashed-out gaps in his teeth, his gooned
eyes gawping at me, brew slishing over the rims
of his lids, hate for the question — "How old are you?" that,
slung back, turns the hope of 18 into an over-30 derision,
the truth slinking him, suddenly aloof, away, hate
that fresh meat is everything, and hate welling for all
the hours of sweating at cranked decibels, ligaments
wrenched, exhaustion seeping for this one slack moment
in the light, not a fucker truly listening, a c-sharp crashing
like a stitch in what was always too slippery to be worn,
gauntlets gouging at my wrists, hair snagged on every
last spike, a self-imposed exercise in obliteration, with
artistic merit — perhaps — hating always the doubt that
dogs all, hate that surety is for the weak — O
and why not hate the praise too?
For it is the same, each time, as though compliments
bleed from a mold and how often can one say "Thanks, man"
before one grows tired enough to mount one's own tall
throne of hate and spit on the minion throngs whose lusts
and loathings sound the same from such perfect distances.

Plazer 2

Love remains for the martyr:
Slither slipping down to the buff, swinging his weeny prick
to Cooper's "I'm Eighteen" on karaoke night, Jasper
ralphing on command, launching into the crowd
with a child's obliviousness of space, or deeper
than this, love for the wrestler turned death metal
singer who systematically enacts a spirit quest
through pain, the flames & tacks, glass & wire

entering his slow, ponderous beauty, love
for his blood as it flecks onto our skin,
a dark priest's censer, love is this extreme,
won't hedge at anything, the abject & the blithe
embraced alike, on this stage, this raw
awakening place, vulnerable as this,
it must be.

Plazer 3

Festival at Avignon, May 2006

Love for the space in which we sang, its stage
the magical demarcation of tape on a common floor.

Love for Kim's wiry bones, his platforms and all Sasha's
80s spray-crazed hair.

For the roster of bands, rough local vermin to hewn
angels, love for this great chain of music!

And efficiency, each act blooming its hard flower in
half hour sets, take down fast, sprung muscles

rafting amps across the span, stacking them like cubes
of air, everywhere cords veining across monitors, taped

against mics, and even when the next band yells —
"Anyone have a spare pedal?" loving the panic

of forgetting the essential and then the rescue
just before the first stunned *plif* from the smoke

machine as buddy grabs the missing gear from his truck
and all is once again fellowship.

Love for the way we play through pain.

Sirventes

"Therefore I shall show and make known what oppresses me."
—GORMONDA DE MONPESLIER

Girls like this (*metal heads*) exist, but are so rare it's useless to
search. There are two things that exist that are similar but not
quite it though. First is the Barbie in disguise—the girl with
no inclination towards metal but dresses up "metal" to either fit
in or impress someone but really hasn't got a metal bone in her
fucking shell. Second is the girl who is actually just a boy with
a vagina and soooometimes a pretty face — sounds alright
doesn't it? Well in fact this is the most annoying breed to me,
because these dames try so fucking hard to be more "metal"
than boys by dressing more "metal," knowing more about the
bands, knowing "deeper" more "underground/kvlt" bands, and
dressing more like fucking boys than boys do. All just to out-
elite the fanboys of the metal scene. "True metal babes" can
only be classified when they actually legitimately are musicians
and into the music. Although EVEN THEN, they may have
only gotten into it and be into it still JUST to out-elite the boys.

Anonymous Facebook post by a male metal musician, 2012.

Part One

Aurillac,
You are innocent, a realm for society's undercurrents
those who will not succumb to the slick glass lands
where the *lauzengiers* ply their trade in lies —
the condemned boutiques, the infernal towers

Aurillac,
You are dark and moldering and bled through with music
to which the initiates dance with stung fury but

Aurillac,
You are no utopia
you have always been infested with the crudest of minds
men who parade women in chains
across the decaying red carpet
until one bursts free to sing
against the rhythm of them seething: "You common whore,
a woman possessed by the devil, a termagant driven by hatred"

O, they have uttered these things
and not only at a roadside club
but in the senates and from the throne
outside Langue d'Oc

Part Two

Aurillac,
Do I answer to you?
are you but the containment of hate
or have your very walls
allowed such sentiments to breed
like black flies in a rutting swamp?

Aurillac,
If I answer their charges of slut,
ball-breaker, fiend,
is that cow still trying to break into the scene

they ask, or kinder yet, your fan base would increase
if more clothes were shed,
if I speak, my voice is said to be whiny or hard, my
complaints absurd — "this is a man's game, doll, if you want
open arms, go and play with the girls"

if I let them know

Aurillac,
of the anxious wreckage of my heart
when I strap on the bass
and how I must strain for the indifference
at the core of fierceness
they will see me as weak
even in my surmounting
insufficient to embody such an art
its cold and unyielding doctrines.

Part Three

Aurillac,
the heresy is this —
that art is sexed

Aurillac,
How could my ache to spend a rhythm, spin it on my
tongue's wheel and set it damp as birth inside the blood of a crowd
be of one shape, one form?
Never since I was a child have I understood
the mind's need to box men and women
like so many broken gifts

when art is,
in its unboundedness,
as blind as love.

Aurillac,
until such fear is crushed
how can art uproot the edifices
erected against you, how
can it silence those laws struck
to strip you down?

Part Four

Aurillac,
You are threatened
and in this we are kin,
the Pope's oath denouncing heretics
manifests in many eras
and Béziers' burning
has left ashes in the minds of its descendants.

The Inquisition resumes

Aurillac,
in the signs of edicts, redevelopments, undercover cops
so with the rain forests, the wilderness of song
is slashed into resource, into absence.
We cannot submit,

Aurillac,
But must strengthen our art
until shame meets its slaughter of singers,
until it acclaims the stage against the stagnant,
Teresias its patron saint, sightless visionary,
deep androgyne,

O, Aurillac,
Pure and corrupt as us all.

Why the Trobairitz Picks Up Men at a Metal Festival

I enter

the Coliseum of Flesh: boys

with elaborate hair & symbolic skin, shirtless and moist

in the whirling bodies around the stage
& take my pick from them all.

How is this wrong.
High-born I proclaim —

monogamy is for those who fear.
To not be owned by a single

set of arms as a moat without a drawbridge
but to hold when I please these men of intensity —

here receiving the sleek bolt of a touch, there
a tongue playing its lightning in my mouth &

moving on in the way of music, finding a song
for it in the morning perhaps, as the boy

sleeps his moment in my bed,

his string-worn fingers sweet.

{ Part Three }

The
Medieval Names
of Metal

Where a Metal Man Stands So Is Summoned a Troubadour

As through the original, medieval eyes of the one, so the borrowed
flails & maces of the other, the romance of serfdom and moats,
the electric fiefs where an eternally buxom wench slides ale upon ale
across the long and mirrored table of history.

As through the one's Langue d'Oc valuation of love, though its fin d'amour
tropes be couched for the castle's ineffable domna, so
the other's guttural rendition of desire, though it be for groupie, as both, no
matter the class, call the feared of sex bitch, bocx,
cons, hottie, res, and each prefer her easy on the eye, endlessly springtime
and, by design, taciturnas.

As through the one's exiled younger sons, denied land and love makers,
not war-mongerers, shamed into itinerant misery, making
the best of it with the bosses' brides, singing sweet of dispossession, so
the other's sons of miners, truckers, spawn of welfare
mothers with their Lipton Soup de Jour and cardboard guitars, becoming
stars in back seats with shit mix and a scrounged pick, besting
that blue collar battle.

As through the tonal modesty of one whose tunes chant humilis from
biology's dominance, who sings of the season's sympathy with his pain
over unattainability, so the other's babe of despair, courted in the realm
of power ballad, chick bent over the bed of a Marshall
stack to assuage manhood's simple doubts, o they are different, but
in couture, not semantics.

As through the one's destruction by edict, Béziers' burning, the vernacular
set aflame and all earthly love a heresy, condemned, so
the other's Dionysian violence, his leather stance, his stage of sweat and
hair shorn for commerce, bars dismantled by the spiffed
bourgeoisie, religion fastened, as always, to control and I, a trobairitz,
ghost of their cosmos, grieving.

A Prayer by Guilhem de Peitieu, circa 1109

Hail Mary, full of *dezir*
let us all be with you
Blessed art you among *puta*
and blessed is the juice of your *cons* —
delicious!
Lovely Mary, mother of *amor*
copulate with us sinners
now and at the hour of our *mort*
Amen

A Prayer by Corpsebanger of Surrey, circa 2008

Bloody Mary, full of shit
Let us all now kill you
Cursed are you among bitches
and cursed is the spawn of your cunt
Jesus.
Lady of Decay, mother of Nothingness
Slay with us now
and until your last breath is thieved from you,
Amen

Metal Lexicon: A Table of Elements

BEER:
De rigeur. Quaffed from a tin or pitcher.
Should be draft.

THE CLUB:
Skanky slice of town. Beer-stuck surfaces;
toilets glutted. Metal-spirit stinking out of amps.

BLACK:
Requisite stark. Dirt earthlings with the devil
in our fabric. You can't go back.

THE HORNS I:
An old Italian woman was the origin. (According to
Dio, little god with big swords. Pipes too.)

TATS:
That's the short form. Don't get it; don't have any.
Symbols of life on the rebel-body.

THE HEADBANG:
Not for nothing was the neck dubbed the most flexible
part. Faster than a double kick. Hair helps.

HAIR:
Heavy head of it essential. Barbarians of the 21st
century. Oiled au naturel.

MOSHING:
Mostly left to punks, more slam-bam than circle-
jerk. Arms crossed, preferred. Reverence, a statue.

WEAPONS:
Rarely guns; anachronisms excite. Battle axes &
flails. Medieval kinds of death.

THE FINGER:
Used less liberally than punks. Punctuating device
for primates. The horns, paramount.

THE NOD:
No junkie's slump. Chin stabbing down, then up.
Cynic's sign of recognition — so what if yr in the club!

SILVER:
Our own personal galaxies. Studs or spikes. Tight-
screwed into the night of our clothes.

THE HORNS 2:
Demon in the hand. Metal's metronome. A sea
of them one sharp testament to intensity.

Metal Show

Tribe is what they are.
Tees bleeding on their backs like rituals, pariah-words:
Pure Uncunted Death, Fuck me Jesus, Butchered at Birth.
They are Nietzschean theory, gutted.

They are raw birds, eyes banged out of their heads
from speed, from sleeplessness, heaving through the door in a
horde, weed jammed under fingernails, mickey up the snatch,
beer slashing in Styrofoam, lines creeping into nostrils

and Blam!

Blamblamblam, they are double-kick bashed by the roadie,
bass hammered, band-spine peeled in sound, *checkcheckcheck*
One two Marshall stacks racked up along the back
phalanx of power streaming through cords shooting

through the mics' nodes they are
reverb overdrive whammy half-cut first note
jabbing their pricks in a needle of music so loud
organs implode hearts unfasten from ventricles

rib-gorged, flesh vibrating until sweat ricochets
like rutting skin, pared of its jean, its hide they
are tattied & pierced, scarred from the pit's
rash clashing of muscle, punt of boot, yank you up

if you slam down, the slatted ground, drink-stuck circle
brutal, the elbow, spiked gauntlet ravaged
across the back but they're
not going to stop, the band prowling its grind,

its scream sheared from the lungs, pieces of blood-
song raking the mind and they are steel,
primal, straining their own wild strings to breaking,
spastic, mad with the lust of it, smoke & lights

in shit-loads, every beat a feast, horrifying,
beautiful, and they are
ringing for weeks afterwards, the whole sea of horns so
kick-ass, such good times, my friends,

Fucking rights.

Gap/Planh for Tendonitis

Athletes of the smallest muscles, we
all know the day when the hand has raced
on the fret board's track, the fingers have strained against the heft
of the strings one too many times and, even before a crowd when
failure's the first bane of sound, give out,

pick slamming to the floor, bass floating away from its beat as
numbness congeals the flesh and, but for grief, we feel nothing
until later when the web between the tendons thrums swollen
and every gesture is ache, can't play, can't work, can't turn a tap,
cannot fathom anymore who we are, divested of such everythings

and so some of us give up, give in, cease the jams, the shows, grow
out of the invincible and, miserable, normal, become merely human
while others seek ways of playing less, playing light, finding the line
between pain & silence, but there are those heroic, those holy
ones that play on despite, the heat never leaving them but like

saints, holding their instruments high, sweat bitter on their skins,
they play.

The Transfiguration

Boot on the monitor, sweat-riven, black
leathered, goat-skinned, one with a wolf's pelt, one
near-naked, inked on as a cave or milk
flesh, steel in the soft parts, guitar, drums, bass
arrayed like runes, hung in pendants, rhythm
tunnelling beneath feet, vibrating up
to where she, her lace, her listening, presses
against him, his camo, his drinking in,
slow, hard sounds the stacks feast them with until
the singer, celebrant, holds court in each
atom, fastens their flawed lives with his music.
Turning to thank him, to shake hands, the show
ended, he is not any longer god
but old-eyed, smeared, just wants a smoke, dinner,
blow job on the bus. Chastened, he passes.

A Singspiel, or, The Rehearsal

In a humble basement room
a band sets up to play their tunes
but before you hear one note, one song
they gather round to hit the bong,
hit the bong.

Aieee aieee yi aiiieeeeee yi!

Then you think they'll start their set
but the cosmos isn't aligned yet
you're missing metal's central point
it's a great excuse to roll a joint,
roll a joint.

Yi heeee haaaa o yaaa haaa ho!

Now the roach is toked to ash
not a riff; the hours have passed
but can one jam without a reefer   NO!
let's take a break and call the dealer
call the dealer.

Hie ya eiiiiiiiiiieeee ya haiya whoo!

Metal Party

7 PM
Everyone wonders why they're here. The beer, yes,
and nebulous, celebratory urges
but we are awkward in the light and the steaks still aren't done.

8 PM
Testament blasts from the deck, darkening
what is common: the table proverbially groaning
with slaw & buns, mutts pumping each other's
hindquarters, a girl rolling out the Slip n Slide
with all the world's six-year-old hopes.

9 PM
Paper plates of gnawings on every surface: meat
& its side dishes. Tasha sips a slushie, part Smirnoff
part mystery. Jimmy downs shit mix with a smiley
face tab, the rest settle for Keiths, cans leaping
like fish from the cooler.

10 PM
Peckerhead shows up, frizzled mop & plumber's
crack flashing as he squats to Zippo the scrap wood,
twists of Sobey flyers. Dave slides in Bathory and
the drunk horns rise, chorus of crusty voices
chanting dragons. Brian's jousting with the door
again. *Always about this time*, someone says,
all chaos fixed in patterns.

11:30 PM

Al's been crashed on the couch for hours now, drool
milking his Carcass hoodie, John hunched over him,
sketching wienies on his face. A pot of shrooms
steams in the kitchen. Lita parades her new tats
around the yard — *the most rad rose and skull ever eh* —
Danny agrees, sneaking glimpses at her tits.
Janna yells from the bathroom — *it's too bright,*
I can't see myself!

12 AM

Tim hands out the brew in teacups: psychedelic
civility. Dreads lashing the weedy air, Denis
moshes with the table, chairs, a dog or two,
Zimmer's Hole ramped up to ten.
Boo-urns! Liza moans, only the stems
left. Scarfs them anyway, waiting for the walls'
lost tribes.

1 AM

Shrooms kicking in — their geriatric distortions.
Teeth & eyes is all there is, Matt proclaims,
woozing his way through the obstacle course
of sudden thinkers. Angel gets horny, slaps
everyone with kisses, her old man passed out
by the fire. Brian whirls on his own wild pivot,
daring the devil to wrestle with him.
Always about this time, the same prophet says,
all party habits charted.

2 AM

Sadie & Frank make out in the bathtub while
Tim unleashes a demon of puke
over the bowl. *Scuse me* Ricky slurs, lurching
through the sheet for a door and pissing
in the sink. *Lil too much togetherness here,*
Tasha announces, hauling up the neckers
by their band tees, turfing them into the hall.
Ow! My fucking lip ring's caught! Bad wall,
bad wall, bad!

3:45 AM

No one is certain how many remain.
Dogs & people leak out of the gates.
Pieces of melon drenched in Johnny Walker
are slurped up by the survivors. Amon Amarth
beats a Viking lament and mouth to mouth
Allie feeds Frank chips, pressing him erect
in the dark. *Lookit, upside down cross!*
Brian gasps at the planks in the still-spitting fire.
Swear, just appeared! Allen headlocks
him good — *nope, can't fool us, bud* — tangles
him to the damp earth while all around the slumping
groups, birds begin their ending.

Ballad of the Metal Men

Refrain:
O I love hanging out with the metal men!
Their company just can't be beat
I love hanging out with the metal men
Each minute a grim, hardcore treat.

Verse the First:
The metal man's home is his castle
Akin to the ruins at Kent
Midst medieval flails there's Kraft Dinner
'Aft Kokanee beer there's no rent!

The furniture's dragged up from the alley
Scarred by cats, dogs and cigarette holes
Chef Boyardee burned to the Bunsen
Graffitteed nude chicks on the walls.

Verse the Second:
The metal man's show is his triumph
His gear a loyal family of sound
Lugged from vans to the stage with persistence
Only four hours to wait for the crowd.

With smoke or with blood or with strobe lights
The most intense show is his aim
Gouging eardrums and gutting your brain cells
Metal's ode to the beauty of pain.

Verse the Third:
The metal man's life is a struggle
Touring & gigging the pit
Where sweaty kids crowd surf off Marshalls
The floor slick with beer, puke & spit.

But there's no other road he'd be missing
Than this black, tattooed loud path he's on
With groupies and brew to console him
Arms fused in a union of horns!

Tribute

(FOR RJD 1942-2010)

Nergal's leukemia bums us out for sure but since
Ronnie James rode his rainbow into darkness it's hard
To get as worked up about the loss of gods.
Others would name Morrison, or Johnny Cash, or Elvis
But for metalheads, Dio was the hero, the man on the Silver
Mountain, the king of singing the diminished 5th, the Italian
Prince of Horns. After the first grief, there will be more, but
None like that descent of the sword into the master's throne,
The knowing he too is blood, that the tiger he rides will no
Longer be in our sight, that this Holy Diver will sing forever
Beyond us of a Heaven & Hell we can't hear.

The End of Metal (2009)

The old man of twenty-four, the drummer, flaunts ear plugs
— *gotta protect the goods* — while the singer trims his shag to
ear-length. *Hey! Why don't we use samples. People love that shit!*
And before you know it the blasts are halved by Leatherface
& Little Nicky, evil Hollywood-style, as the guitarist breaks it
down for you on the keys, sharing his feelings about high
school. Selling out in the basement ain't for wimps. Book a
show but the venue burns to the ground and re-opens as a
hip-hop club or narcs snatch its license. They nearly play a gig
until Steve becomes a crackhead, Jay breaks his leg boarding,
John goes on a shutdown, Larry pegs Tim's woman. The
girlfriends run the gossip mills, distribute backyard tabloids.
So & so's a slut, a lush, a ho, a skank, a backstabber, a fruit, all
high n mighty, a shithead, a dickface, a fattie, loosey-goosey,
two-timer, bitch. Selling out in the alleyway ain't for losers.
Dan starts to chill with Dream Theatre instead of Slayer,
Tom thinks the new Metallica's "not bad." It's all about the
merch anyway: bullet belts for pacifists, vests with cell phone
pockets, all that camo to play video games in. *Anyone got Rock
Band 13, man, it's really like you're virtually on stage!* Terry keeps
working late, Mandy drinks til she shits her pleathers, Clay
gets too baked to stay awake after nine, Barry does acid and
forgets all the songs. No one can talk about anyone but when
they're not there; no one can talk to each other without a
You're fucking dead! In the empty jam space, the Ibanez looks so
cool, the custom Warlock wicked.

Part Four

An
Ineffable Travelogue
in Two Prose Poems
(2007)

The Invisibility of Troubadours

I was having a quiet competition with the troubadours
and they were winning. It should have seemed likely.
After all, they were dead and I, well, I was still somewhat
alive, if half famished on my ten Euro a day diet.
Everywhere I went in Provence I had asked, in the
timorous, yet persistent, tone of a misplaced tourist,
"Est-ce-que il y'a des troubadours ici?"
I quested for them at the Palais des Papes in Avignon,
wondered about them with a bus driver wending me to
Le Mas de Micocouliers in Aix, and demanded their
whereabouts of two scruff-haired punks at the Jardins
des Poetes in Béziers. More promisingly, I squatted on
the parapets of Carcassonne Castle for hours, hoping to
hear the spectral strains of Peire Cardenal's "Ar me pulsc"
but caught only the commentary of tour guides
expostulating on the ins & outs of medieval lavatories. I
even allowed a portly little framer I had encountered on
the train to taxi me to Aigues Morts in Montpellier,
enduring the plop of his hand on my thigh in order to
scent out the potential of trobairitzes. Perhaps they were
hiding behind the pigeon-shat statue of King Louis,
standing staunch above his monstrous dolphin cohort
whose dry basin played host to a farrago of knuckled-in
beer cans. Nada. Marseilles exuded a turbulent
theatricality that tasted somewhat of the scarcely-

restrained eroticism simmering in many of the fin d'amour cansos. Orange proffered a bust of Raimbaut d'Orange, one that, on disappointed inspection, proved to be that of the town's viscount and not the troubadour; Raimbaut as ubiquitous a name in that era as John or Chris is in our own. That was all. Alas. Or should I say Hélas! Had I come this far to merely trog from hostel to hostel, often lost, subsisting on a petit dejeuner a day, troubadour-bereft? How had I forgotten that they were poets, anonymous, and eventually anomalies, in royal retinues or, if regal themselves, as with the case of their female counterparts, secretive in their pursuit of song, the joglars the voice of their tensons or plazers. Why was I tracing the dust of a tune in this land where only the warriors were commemorated and Langue d'Oc had become little more than a eucalyptus seed skirling in the mistral by the empty Mediterranean sea.

The Ubiquitous Troubadours

At the Tulip Hostel, in the Beyoglu district of Istanbul, Turkey, I finally met what I thought were the origins of troubadour verse in the modern guise of five young Moroccan men: Mohammed, Nabil, Mahsud, Karim and Zach. They spoke Arabic, the language lodged at the courtly crux of the genre, its guttural lucidity flowing through Moorish Spain to commingle with the vernacular glottals of Langue d'Oc. They also spoke French, the medium through which we talked. Tight of jean, dark of lock, their eyes were liquid with the ancient rituals of mysterious courtship.

*

On the second day of my stay, they invited me to lunch with them, Mohammed quickly assembling a potato dish with sliced tomatoes; I scooping up the soft feast with crescents of bread, washing it all down with whisky, Coke and rakı. After the meal, they popped a tape of Arabic tunes into the 80s ghetto blaster and showed me how to dance like a Moroccan man: hands on hips, pelvis rolling, head frothing in the rhythmic heat. I couldn't have been more enchanted. These petits troubadours were my medieval brothers, my chaste and holy senhals.

*

But when the tape stopped, Nabil grabbed my hand and yanked me towards the stairs, claiming that he wanted to show me something. And apparently that something was located *dans ma chambre.* I protested; he countered. *"Mais la premiere fois que je t'ai vue, c'est comme il y avait un papillon dans ma coeur. J'ai les yeux seulement pour toi."* Well, he had the rhetoric down at least; the tropes of butterflies and devotion were bang on. Yet things weren't supposed to proceed at such a pell-mell pace, complete with him compelling an instantaneous groin caress...

*

My research hadn't been careful enough. Arab courtly love poets, my *Histoire de les Troubadours* later reminded me, had constructed tropes designed to "possess, rather than venerate the object of desire." My petits troubadours were merely carrying on a strangely venerable tradition while I had lunged centuries ahead, to other courts entirely, where I was serenaded harmlessly from below the negligible window of opportunity in the highest tower.

Part Five

Postscript

The Death of the Troubadours: An Apologia

I'm sure you've heard of killing what one claims to love. Well this is it. Worse than the inferno at Béziers ordered by Pope Innocent to slay the Cathars and other earthly heretics. Crueller than the Inquisition's 1209 edict of silence. Increasingly omnipotent, unlike the cult of the Virgin Mary that knocked courtly adoration heavenward, twisting the *Midons* into Mother.

No, the exiled might have fled this: the ashes, the pledge, even the church, emerging again in Trieste, Barcelona, Madrid, singing.

But the Occitanian courts were gone, eviscerated by endless Crusades and with them, Langue d'Oc. French surged into an ascendancy that only English has been able to rout and, most damningly, the oral culture receded into books — fixed, legitimate, quelled.

This then is what I've continued to fulfill. Freezing what was fluid, ineffable in one archetypal man, one troubadour of metal and a trobairitz without a castle, speaking the song that oppressed her oppressors. Enabling the further death of their songs.

All wrong.
Though what else, once I heard that tune, could I have done.

Canso of a Thousand Years Hence

Dearest Senhal, I don't know what you want of me,
to forget you, perhaps, or worse,
nothing.

Still, after all these centuries, seeing a picture of you
sends me, painfully, through the seasons.
Spring,

its brisk green ache, summer's red memories, the sharp
indifference of autumn, and always, finally, to the
longest

time of year in which your heart, once hidden, is buried once
again, as if (always as if) forever, in the snow of an image
snapped

by another domna, and another, and yet a third,
none of them able to sing of your music as she
who

in fear, in claiming, or worse, for no
such reason at all, you once
spurned.

Reprise: Two Years Later

In the last dream I had of you Senhal,
you were mine in perpetuity,
a reverie absurd as my attachment
to this land.
In the dream you renounced others,
embraced me, had tears in your eyes
as "finally," you said, "forever"
though in life the last gesture you would make
is a sentimental one, the last thing
I would see you do is cry.
No, Senhal, these dreams are lies
and are painful to me, my mind
creating Edens where in truth
the birds fall silent from poisons
and there are many kinds of ice
on the river.

Return: Three Years After

When will it end, you're the curse of my soul
—DOKKEN "Into the Fire"

canso (again)

Once more the storm
with its ache of hard rain, its burning
turbulence of light.

How did I forget, even for an instant,
this place where the violence of your sky
enters me and there are

no years between us, Senhal.
I stand beneath you and am nearly
drowned in the sweet unhallowed

thunder of our blood.

Villanelle

As if in a dream, we were already there
The woods of Calais, the park at Béziers
And after, the autumn you stroked from my hair.

Though it was still summer, the sun burning fair
Then the star-less night sky, its darkness so clear.
When, as if in a dream, we were already there

The woods of Printemps, the park of Hiver
Where you held me as though we had little to fear
Then, gentle, the autumn you drew from my hair.

After the hour that our flesh was held bare,
We were both now as far, we were both just as near
As if in a dream we were already there

In the woods of Alsace, the park at Beaucaire,
You speaking the words I'd long wanted to hear
While the autumn you stopped to caress from my hair

Spun down to the pavement, blew wild in the square
As we left the freed woods, the park without care
Where, as if in a dream, we were already there
And, always, the autumn, your hands in my hair.

Canso of As It Is

"for one man is my world of all the men"
—CHRISTINA ROSETTI

Still strange this land, always:
beautiful, ruthless, brutal by turn
and never does it cease speaking to me
of exile, from you,

Senhal, from the ocean, its shadows of salt,
its wild, unclaimable tides, but I can do
nothing more than I have and be
no one more than I am,

cannot run from my liege into your arms, which,
like the wind through this field, would not be
changed by my embraces, not saved, not
returned home,

no, they would hold me just a while from desire,
then leave me to grow old.

Five Years Past the First Time

Canso of Forever

In ten years, you write me,
let's go away from each other, not see
each other age, grow ill, not watch
our demise.
In this way, perhaps, we'll have some
relief.

You tell me this,
after all the poems I've given you,
poems in which you are myth,
a troubadour of metal, immutable,
too beautiful to be real.

It is you who thinks you will become
less with time
when you are the one who will always
survive in me, transcendent.
What I will be to you when old
I cannot think of.

What have I ever been.

To the Immortal One

You, the muse who has survived so many poems & who
continues to exist outside medieval worlds,

who has become words from flesh and yet who persists
as flesh beyond words so that when I stand beside you

in a place far from all castles I am still drawn to you
& how beautifully do not long for what came before

but am calm just standing arm to arm, feeling you
breathing, knowing you're alive.

Glossary of Terms

Alba: *Dawn song vs. the pastorelas which was a misogynistic ditty about shepherdesses.*

Amic: *friend.*

Aurillac: *A town in the south of France in which trobairitzes and troubadours recited, as with the other towns in Trobairitz such as Avignon, Dauphiné and Saintonge. While the latter names invoke meaningful regions for the modern day Comtessa and her Senhal Fohlia, Aurillac is the pseudonym for a metal club where both these contemporary troubadours play. Aurillac is also the subject of the sirventes form poem, a site that symbolizes the contradictions of being an underground artist functioning within frequently misogynistic conventions.*

Bels Deportz: *Lovely Lady or Nice View. Could be dismissive.*

Béziers: *A Langue d'Oc stronghold of Catharism, which the Catholic Church condemned as heretical and which Catholic forces exterminated in the Albigensian Crusade of 1209.*

Bosphorus: *Also known as the Istanbul Strait, the body of water that forms part of the boundary between Europe and Asia.*

Canso: *The courtly love poem whose traditional structure can be found in the poem Comjat.*

Canso 23: *This canso is in traditional alba form. The alba was a piece sung at dawn. During the time of the trobairitzes it was performed as a mode of opposition to the more conventional pastorela, or country song, quite frequently a misogynistic ditty about shepherdesses.*

Chansonniers: *Medieval songbooks.*

Comjat: *A poem that expresses leave taking; as previously mentioned, this is the only canso in traditional form.*

Cons: *Quite simply, cunt.*

Countess of Dia: *An actual trobairitz as well as the heroine of the cansos.*

Her real biography, along with that of the other trobairitzes, from whom quotes have been drawn, can be found in Meg Bogin's key text: *The Women Troubadours*. Other essential texts were Paden's *The Voice of the Troubadours* and Gaunt & Kay's *The Troubadours: An Introduction*.

DEVINALH: *Riddle poem.*

DEZIR/PUTA *(whore)*/AMOR/CONS *(cunt)*: *Words of lust that would have been used in such bawdy songs to Mary.*

DOMNA: *The lady, usually married to the lord. However, in this case, as the muse for the Comtessa is male, he is often referred to as the Domna, making him interchangeable with his lady.*

EN/NA: *Lord & Lady.*

ENEUG/PLAZER: *Lists of what one hates/loves.*

ESCONDIG: *A lover's apology.*

FALS D'AMOUR: *A mockery of fin d'amour or troubadour love songs.*

FORFEITZ/MARRITZ/FALHIR: *All terms connoting various kinds of failure in love.*

GAP/PLANH: *A complaint form/A bragging form.*

GARDADORS: *A lady's chaperones or guardians.*

GILEOS: *Jealous one. Rival.*

JOGLAR/JOGLARESA: *Performers of troubadour verse who weren't creators of the genre themselves. Thus often a pejorative term.*

LANGUE D'OC: *The Occitanian language of the medieval troubadours.*

MEZURA: *Balance in love.*

MIDONS: *Lord. A term curiously often used for the lady the troubadour was wooing.*

MIELS DE DOMNA: *My only Lady. My best one.*

NEMRUT DAGI (*pronounced Da-hu*) *is a mountain in southeastern Turkey, notable for the many statues scattered around the summit, including one of Heracles, the Greek god.*

NEUMES: *A musical term that measures notations of pitch without accounting for time.*

PARTIMEN: *A small play text for multiple voices.*

RAZO: *A short composition detailing the origins, both biographical and historical, of the poem/song.*

RES: *Thing.*

SENHAL FOHLIA: *A pseudonym akin to the kind often invoked in troubadour verse. In this case, Senhal actually means pen name and Fohlia is a term that expresses the madness of love.*

SINGSPIEL: *Medieval song-play.*

SIRVENTES: *A political poem. The first part states the issue. The second part complicates the problem. The third part makes the heresy or lie behind this conflict explicit. The fourth part attempts to find a resolution. This piece addresses the metal club in personified fashion, asking whether it is ally or enemy to the Comtessa's quest for equality in the predominantly male scene.*

TACITURNAS: *An admirable quality in a woman, the art of keeping silent.*

TENSON/TENSO: *A debate or argument poem between two voices/perspectives.*

TORNADA: *A self-referential gesture common at the end of a canso.*

TROBAR CLUS: *A closed, difficult to fathom, hermetic form of verse.*

VIDA: *A brief synopsis of a troubadour's biography*

"A VOS MAS COBLAS MAN": *To you my stanzas go. Or so says the Comtessa to her Senhal's Lady, trying to assuage her own guilt and the Domna's jealousy.*

ACKNOWLEDGMENTS

"Amor de Lonh"
The Dalhousie Review

"The Transfiguration"
Poetry is Dead

Six of the Cansos appear in a chapbook from The Olive Press (AB) titled *13 Lovers* (2007).

Sources

Bogin, Meg. *The Women Troubadours*. London: Paddington, 1976

Christe, Ian. *Sound of the Beast: A Complete Headbanging History of Heavy Metal*. New York: Harper Collins/Harper Entertainment, 2004.

Gaunt, Simon & Sarah Kay. *The Troubadours: An Introduction*. Cambridge: Cambridge University Press, 1999.

Paden, William D. ed. *The Voice of the Trobairitz: Perspectives on the Women Troubadours*. Philadelphia: University of Pennsylvania Press, 1989.

Weinstein, Deena. *Heavy Metal: The Music & its Culture*. New York: Da Capo Press, 2000.

ABOUT THE AUTHOR

CATHERINE OWEN is a Vancouver poet and writer, the author of nine collections of poetry. A book of essays and memoirs, *Catalysts: Confrontations with the Muse*, was published earlier this year. Catherine's work has appeared in periodicals throughout Canada, Austria, New Zealand, and Australia. Her books and poems have been nominated for numerous awards, including the Gerald Lampert Award, the BC Book Prize, the ReLit Award, the George Ryga Award for Social Awareness in Literature, Short Grain, and The Earle Birney Prize. Her last book of poetry, *Frenzy* (Anvil), won the Alberta Literary Award in 2010. She has a Masters degree in English and played bass in the metal bands Inhuman and Helgrind. Her current metal project is Medea.